LET'S GO TO THE MOVIES!
A Collection of Tales, Trivia, and Quotes

by
Lester Gordon

SANTA MONICA PRESS
P.O. Box 1076
Santa Monica, CA 90406-1076
Printed in the United States
All Rights Reserved

TABLE OF CONTENTS

FASCINATING FACTS ABOUT THE MOVIES AND YOUR FAVORITE STARS

ONCE UPON A TIME . . .

Margaret Hamilton, who was so perfectly evil as the Wicked Witch of the West in *The Wizard of Oz*, was once a kindergarten teacher.

Humphrey Bogart's slight lisp was a result of an injury he received during World War II. While his ship was being shelled, a splinter lodged in his upper lip, rendering it paralyzed.

Before moving to Hollywood together, Stan Laurel was Charlie Chaplin's understudy on the English stage. Once in America, the two friends shared a room in a boardinghouse. Cooking was not allowed, so Chaplin would play the violin to cover up the sound of Laurel frying up food on a hot plate.

Robert Mitchum was once confined to a chain gang for seven days.

Gene Hackman and Dustin Hoffman were voted least likely to succeed by their classmates at the Playhouse Acting School.

Lou Costello — the heavy partner of Abbott — was once a boxer.

Bob Hope was also once a boxer, fighting under the name of Packy East.

Johnny Weissmuller, famous as Tarzan, was a 1924 Olympic swimming gold medalist.

Doris Day originally longed to be a professional dancer, but when she broke her leg at the age of fifteen, she decided to give singing a try.

Lucille Ball was kicked out of drama school for being too shy.

Before he became a movie star, W.C. Fields earned money as a professional "drowner" in Atlantic City, New Jersey. A concession stand owner would send Fields into the ocean, where he would pretend to drown. While someone rescued the future comedian and began reviving him on the beach, a crowd would gather, and the concessionaire would sell snacks and soft drinks to the curious people watching the action.

CASTING CALLS

Upon noticing that Charlton Heston's nose was broken in the same place as where Michelangelo's statue of Moses has his nose broken, Cecil B. DeMille hired the actor for the remake of *The Ten Commandments* (1956).

Ronald Reagan was once the front runner for the role of Rick in *Casablanca* (1942).

Marlon Brando was once the front runner for the title role in *Lawrence of Arabia* (1963).

Bette Davis, Susan Hayward, and Paulette Goddard were among the many actresses who were turned down for the part of Scarlett O'Hara in *Gone With the Wind* (1939). Vivien Leigh, who was ultimately given the role, was brought to the set by the producer's brother.

Clint Eastwood was originally offered the role in *Apocalypse Now!* (1979) that ultimately went to Martin Sheen.

Shirley Temple was originally slated to play the role of Dorothy in *The Wizard of Oz* (1939), but Judy Garland got the part when Temple's studio (20th Century Fox) requested too much money from MGM.

SCREEN TEST TRIVIA

After Fred Astaire completed his first screen test, the report read, "Can't act, slightly bald, can dance a little."

1,400 actresses were interviewed for the role of Scarlett O'Hara and 90 were given screen tests. All told the cost of the search was $92,000.

At the time she received her contract, thirteen year old Judy Garland was the only person in the history of MGM to be signed up without first having completed a screen test.

Clark Gable's first screen test was a failure because it was thought that his ears were too big.

DAZZLING DEBUTS

Liza Minnelli, daughter of Vincent Minnelli and Judy Garland, made her motion picture debut when she was just 2 1/2 years old in the film *The Good Old Summertime* (1946).

Robert Blake, known to millions as *Baretta*, began his acting career by appearing in the *Our Gang* comedies of the '30s. He also had a small role in *The Treasure of Sierra Madre* (1948), when he sold Humphrey Bogart a winning lottery ticket.

Jack Nicholson made his film debut in Roger Corman's *The Cry Baby Killer* (1964).

A NIGHT AT THE OSCARS

Walt Disney was given one normal Oscar statue and seven miniature statues for his film, *Snow White and the Seven Dwarfs* (1937).

Walt Disney has won the most Academy Awards, 26 (plus six special Oscars).

Five actors have won Best Actor awards more than once: Marlon Brando (*On the Waterfront* and *The Godfather*), Gary Cooper (*Sergeant York* and *High Noon*), Dustin Hoffman (*Kramer vs Kramer* and *Rain Man*), Fredric March (*Dr Jekyll and Mr Hyde* and *The Best Years of Our Lives*), and Spencer Tracy (*Captains Courageous* and *Boys Town*).

Ben Hur (1959) won the most awards ever for a single film. It's eleven Oscars included: Best Picture, Best Director, Best Actor, Best Supporting Actor, Sound, Art Direction, Cinematography, Editing, Special Effects, Best Score, and Costumes.

It Happened One Night (1934), *One Flew Over the Cuckoo's Nest* (1976), and *The Silence of the Lambs* (1991) are the only films to have swept all five major awards (Best Picture, Best Director, Best Screenplay, Best Actor, and Best Actress).

Only one Western has ever won the Academy Award for Best Picture: *Cimarron* (1931).

John Ford's four Best Director awards are the most by an individual in that category. They are for the films, *The Informer* (1935), *The Grapes of Wrath* (1940), *How Green Was My Valley* (1941), and *The Quiet Man* (1952).

Katherine Hepburn has won four Best Actress awards, the most by a female performer. The films were: *Morning Glory* (1933), *Guess Who's Coming to Dinner* (1967), *The Lion in Winter* (1968), and *On Golden Pond* (1981).

Anthony Quinn's eight minute performance as Gauguin in *Lust For Life* (1956) is the shortest to ever win an Oscar (he won for Best Supporting Actor).

Tatum O'Neal is the youngest performer to ever win an Academy Award. She was 9 years old when she took home the Oscar for *Paper Moon* (1973). It should be noted that Shirley Temple received a special award for outstanding contribution to screen entertainment when she was only six years old.

The oldest performer to win an Oscar is Jessica Tandy, 80 years 8 months, for her appearance in *Driving Miss Daisy* (1989).

The first black Academy Award winner was Hattie McDaniel, who played Mammy in *Gone With the Wind* (1939). It would be 24 years before another black performer won an Academy Award — Sidney Portier for *Lilies of the Field* (1963).

Spencer Tracy returned his 1938 Best Actor award to the Academy because the statue had been erroneously engraved with the name, "Dick Tracy."

Charlie McCarthy — Edgar Bergen's dummy — received the only wooden Oscar in the history of the Academy Awards for his performance in *The Goldwyn Follies* (1938).

The only X-rated film to ever win an Oscar for Best Picture was *Midnight Cowboy* (1969). The rating was later changed to "R."

The 1972 Academy Awards will be remembered as the time Marlon Brando sent up an Apache Native American to accept his Oscar for best actor. It was later revealed that, true to Hollywood, the woman was actually a little known actress who had been named "Miss American Vampire of 1970."

Highly respected screenwriter Robert Towne, who was upset at the changes that were made to his script for *Greystoke: The Legend of Tarzan, Lord of the Apes* (1984), replaced his name in the credits with that of P.H. Vazak — the name of his Hungarian sheepdog. The dog was later nominated for an Academy Award.

DOLLARS AND SENSE

American Graffiti (1973) cost only $775,000 to make, and went on to earn nearly $40 million.

The most successful film of a live concert is *Eddie Murphy Raw* (1987), which grossed some $50 million.

The Wizard of Oz cost a little over $3 million dollars to make.

The largest publicity budget was $48.1 million for *Dick Tracy*.

Terminator 2, Judgement Day, is the most expensive film ever made at $104 million. *Cleopatra*, however, which cost $44 million in 1963, would cost $186 million in 1990 dollars.

The average budget for a film in 1990 was $18.1 million.

Elizabeth Taylor's wardrobe for *Cleopatra* cost $198,800 — the most ever spent on one performer's costume.

The film *Legal Eagles* used $10 million worth of paintings and sculptures in the scenes set in an art gallery.

Darth Vader's Star Destroyer in *Star Wars* cost $100,000 and features over 250,000 portholes.

The replica of a Spanish galleon in Roman Polanski's *Pirates* (1986) cost more than $13 million, the most ever spent on a single prop.

The highest grossing animated film in the history of the movies is *Snow White and the Seven Dwarfs* (1937).

MOGULS, THEN AND NOW

Sam Warner, who died the day before *The Jazz Singer* premiered, never knew how much the film he was responsible for changed the motion picture industry.

Steven Speilberg and George Lucas are the two most successful producers in the history of cinema. Between them, they have nine films which have grossed over $100 million.

MEMORABLE MEMORABILIA

Three sets of hoof prints grace the cement in front of Grauman's Chinese Theatre in Hollywood — Champion (Gene Autry's horse), Tony (Tom Mix's horse), and Trigger (Roy Rogers' horse).

Judy Garland's ruby slippers from *The Wizard of Oz* (1939) sold for $165,000 at an auction in 1988. The previous year, Charlie Chaplin's bowler and cane were sold for $150,000.

Steven Speilberg paid $60,500 for the Rosebud sled from *Citizen Kane* (1941).

The fishing cap worn by Henry Fonda in *On Golden Pond* (1981) actually belonged to Spencer Tracy. Katherine Hepburn gave Fonda the hat on the first day on the set.

MOVIE NUTS AND BOLTS

The famous shower scene in Alfred Hitchcock's *Psycho* (1960) consisted of 70 different camera shots and lasts 45 seconds.

Because they could not find sharks big enough to suit their needs, the producers of *Jaws* (1975) hired a four foot nine inch ex-jockey to stand inside a scaled-down shark cage, thus making the shark look much bigger than it actually was.

Hollywood's first Western, *The Great Train Robbery* (1903), was actually filmed in New Jersey.

The average number of letters used in the title of a film is 17.

The terrific ending for *Casablanca* was kept a secret through the shoot. Nobody, not even Humphrey Bogart and Ingrid Bergman, knew how the film was going to end until the final scene was ready to be shot.

During close-ups of Bela Lugosi in *Dracula* (1931), flashlights were shone into the actor's eyes to give them an eerie effect.

SPECIAL EFFECTS

The boots that Charlie Chaplin ate in *The Gold Rush* (1924) were made out of licorice.

When Linda Blair vomited in *The Exorcist* (1973), the substance was made out of split pea soup and oatmeal.

The animated dwarfs in *Snow White and the Seven Dwarfs* (1937) were modeled on real people.

Windows in movies are often made out of clear sugar, especially when an actor is going to jump through one.

Charlie Chaplin invented his tramp costume with the help of Fatty Arbuckle's pants, Arbuckle's father-in-law's derby, Chester Cockline's cutaway, Ford Sterling's size 14 shoes, and some crepe paper belonging to Mack Swain (which became the tramp's moustache). The only item that belonged to Chaplin was the whangee cane.

Over 22 million bees were used in *The Swarm* (1978).

The blood in the infamous shower scene from *Psycho* (1960) was actually chocolate sauce.

MOVIES AND MUSIC

The best selling record of a song from a film is "White Christmas," the Irving Berlin tune sung by Bing Crosby in *Holiday Inn* (1942).

The best selling soundtrack from a film is John Williams' score for *Star Wars* (1977).

John Williams is the most successful film composer, having written the score for eight of the ten highest earning movies in history — *Jaws* (1975), *Star Wars* (1977), *The Empire Strikes Back* (1980), *Raiders of the Lost Ark* (1981), *E.T.* (1982), *Return of the Jedi* (1983), *Indiana Jones and the Temple of Doom* (1984), and *Indiana Jones and the Last Crusade* (1989).

TITLES, CREDITS, & ALL THAT JAZZ

Woody Allen originally wanted to title *Annie Hall* (1977), "Anhedonia" — a Greek medical term for someone who can't experience pleasure. Other titles he considered were "Anxiety" and "Annie and Alvy."

The title says, *Krakatoa, East of Java* (1968), but Krakatoa is really 200 miles west of Java.

743 names were credited on *Who Framed Roger Rabbit* (1989) — the most ever.

The screenplay credit for *The Taming of the Shrew* (1929) said, "Written by William Shakespeare. Additional dialogue by Sam Taylor."

THE MOST POPULAR STORY ON FILM

Cinderella is the story which has been remade the most — some 94 times! This includes cartoons, ballet, opera, pornographic, and parody versions.

BANNED!

Prince Rainier has banned all of Grace Kelly's films from being shown in Monaco.

Iraq banned karate films in 1979.

Romania banned Mickey Mouse films in 1935 because the animated character was thought to be frightening to children.

INSURING BODY PARTS

Fred Astaire's legs were once insured for $1 million dollars. Betty Grable's legs were once insured for a bit more money — $1.25 million dollars.

Jimmy Durante once copyrighted his nose. He also had it insured by Lloyd's of London for $100,000 dollars.

HUMOROUS HITCHCOCK

Alfred Hitchcock always managed to make a brief appearance in his films. However, for *Lifeboat* (1944), he was faced with a difficult problem — the entire movie was set in a lifeboat out at sea, and there were only a few characters in the boat. His ingenious solution was to place a photograph of himself in a newspaper one of the characters reads during the course of the film. He can be seen in the "before" portion of a before and after ad for a diet product.

LONGEST, LARGEST, BEST, MOST . . .

Lillian Gish has the longest movie career of any actress, having debuted as a 19 year old in *An Unseen Enemy* (1912), and making her last appearance in *Whales of August* (1987).

The longest kiss recorded on film occurs between Cary Grant and Ingrid Bergman in Alfred Hitchcock's *Notorious* (1946).

When Walt Disney Productions released *Return to Oz* in 1985, it represented the longest time span that had ever occurred between the original and the remake of a film.

At one time, the line "Let's get outta here" had been used in 84% of Hollywood movie productions.

The largest outdoor film set ever built was the Roman Forum used in *The Fall of the Roman Empire* (1964). It was 1,312 feet long by 754 feet wide, took 1,100 workers seven months to construct, and rose some 260 feet in the air.

The largest indoor film set ever built was the landing site for the UFO in *Close Encounters of the Third Kind* (1977). Constructed inside a 10 million cubic foot hangar in Mobile, Alabama, it was 450 feet long by 250 feet wide and was 90 feet tall.

When stuntman and parachutist Dar Robinson leaped from the ledge of the 1,170 foot high CN Tower in Toronto, he was paid $150,000, the most ever for a single stunt.

Tom Wolfe was paid $5 million for the film rights to his novel, *Bonfire of the Vanities*, the most ever earned by an author.

Charlie Chaplin once reshot a scene in *City Lights* (1931) some 342 times before he felt he had gotten it right. In *Some Like It Hot* (1959), Marilyn Monroe required 59 takes on a scene in which her only line was "Where's the Bourbon?" Similarly, Stanley Kubrick required Shelley Duval to redo a scene 127 times in The Shining (1980).

Screenwriter Joe Ezterhas was paid $3 million for his script, *Basic Instinct*, the highest amount ever paid to a screenwriter.

John Hughes wrote the script for *Weird Science* (1985) in two days. He wrote *The Breakfast Club* (1984) in three days, and *National Lampoon's Vacation* (1983) in four days.

Sherlock Holmes is the most portrayed character on film, having been played by 72 actors in 204 films. The historical character most represented in films is Napoleon Bonaparte, with 194 film portrayals. Abraham Lincoln is the U.S. President to be portrayed most on film, with 136 films featuring actors playing the role.

FLUBS

Indiana Jones and the Last Crusade (1989) is riddled with mistakes. At the beginning of the film, Indiana Jones crosses the Atlantic by airliner even though it is 1938 — one year before the first transatlantic passenger service began. In the airport lounge, two people are reading German newspapers that are dated 1918, 20 years before the year in which the film is set. Finally, the "Republic" of Hatay is ruled by someone referred to as "Your Royal Highness."

DID YOU KNOWN THAT...

When she performed for the troops during World War II, Marlene Dietrich would entertain the men by playing the musical saw.

One of the reasons Lon Chaney was such an effective silent film star, was because he had been raised by deaf-mute parents, thus enhancing his ability to relate emotions and actions without the use of sound.

Two hippopotami were present at the second wedding of Elizabeth Taylor and Richard Burton.

After Clark Gable opened his shirt to reveal a bare chest in *It Happened One Night* (1934), sales of undershirts fell nearly 40 percent.

In a 1990 poll of film critics and film makers, *Citizen Kane* (1941) was voted the greatest film ever made. It is worth noting that *Citizen Kane* was a box office flop when it was first released, and that it won only a single Academy Award.

The first screen kiss came in the film, *The Widow Jones*, in 1896. A reviewer at the time described it as "absolutely disgusting." The first French kiss in a Hollywood film occurred in *Splendor in the Grass* (1961), between Natalie Wood and Warren Beatty.

Cedric Gibbons (1893-1960) has the distinction of having had his name appear on the credits of over 1500 films. His 1924 contract stated that every film released by MGM in the USA would give him the credit of Art Director, even though others did the majority of the work.

In 1914, Charlie Chaplin made an astounding 35 movies.

Bela Lugosi, famous for his role as Dracula, was buried in his character's cloak.

In the film, *The Godfather* (1972), Marlon Brando, who often does not learn his lines for a film, had to have his lines written out for him and placed on various locations around the set.

Mel Blanc, the voice of Bugs Bunny and many other beloved cartoon characters, hated carrots. Whenever he was recording the sound track for Bugs, he would keep a bucket next to him where he could spit out the carrots that Bugs was known for eating.

After being unemployed for many years following his starring role in the *Our Gang* series, Spanky McFarland placed the following ad in a Hollywood trade magazine: "Childhood (3-16) spent as leader of *Our Gang* comedies. Won't someone give me the opportunity to make a living in the business I love and know so well? Have beanie, will travel."

Mae West wrote the majority of her film dialogue.

Humphrey Bogart was known to cure a hangover by getting drunk all over again. In fact, he formed his own drinking club, The Holmby Hills Rat Pack, which included his wife Lauren Bacall, David Niven, Judy Garland, John Huston, Adlai Stevenson, Peter Lorre, John O'Hara, and Frank Sinatra.

Liza Minnelli, daughter of Judy Garland, married Jack Haley, Jr., son of Jack Haley, who played The Tin Man.

Shelly Winters performed her own swimming stunts in *The Poseidon Adventure*.

W.C. Fields, jealous of co-star Baby LeRoy, once spiked the child's bottle with liquor. The shooting for the day had to be called off because of the child's drunkenness.

Robert Redford has broken his nose at least five times.

Tom Cruise may have looked good in uniform for *Top Gun* (1986), but in reality, he could have never become a naval pilot — the Navy requires that officers be 5 feet 10 inches tall, and Cruise is only 5 foot 9 inches tall.

Lauren Bacall appears to sing in *To Have and Have Not* (1944), but her voice was actually dubbed — by none other than Andy Williams!

FAMOUS QUIPS
AND QUOTES

ON ACTING AND ACTORS

"Acting is all about honesty. If you can fake that you've got it made."

— *George Burns*

"I've got the celluloid in my blood."

— *W.C. Fields*

"I never said, 'I want to be alone.' I only said, 'I want to be left alone.'"

— *Greta Garbo*

"[MGM] had us working days and nights on end. They'd give us pep-up pills to keep us on our feet long after we were exhausted. Then they'd take us to the studio hospital and knock us cold with sleeping pills . . . Then after four hours they'd wake us up and give us the pep-up pills again so we could work another seventy-two hours in a row."

— *Judy Garland*

"You spend all your life trying to do something they put people in asylums for."

— *Jane Fonda*

"I enjoy being a highly overpaid actor."
— *Roger Moore*

"Why do you throw away five hundred dollars of our money on a test for that big ape? Didn't you see those big ears when you talked to him? And those big feet and hands, not to mention that ugly face of his?"
— *Jack Warner, to Mervyn LeRoy after the latter had given Clark Gable screen test*

"They never had my advantages. I started out poor."
— *Kirk Douglas, referring to his sons.*

"Until forty-five I can still play a woman in love. After fifty-five I can play grandmothers. But between those ten years it is difficult for an actress."
— *Ingrid Bergman*

"Days off."
— *Spencer Tracy, when asked what he looks for in a script*

"Chanel No. 5."
— *Marilyn Monroe, when asked by the press what she wears to bed*

"The only thing you owe the public is a good performance."

— *Humphrey Bogart*

"My only problem is finding a way to play my fortieth fallen female in a different way from my thirty ninth."

— *Barbara Stanwyck*

"Talk low, talk slow, and don't say too much."

— *John Wayne, offering advice on acting*

"Why waste my time and your money? I've tried movie work often enough to know I have nothing Hollywood wants."

— *a discouraged Clark Gable in the early days of his career, speaking to a talent scout*

"With an American actor becoming an actor is rather like a lady becoming a nun. Whereas with an English actor, it's like becoming a plumber."

— *Michael Caine*

"How to become an old actor."

— *Henry Fonda, on the most crucial thing a young actor must learn*

"To me, a Clint Eastwood picture is one that I'm in."

> — *Clint Eastwood, when asked to define the quintessential Clint Eastwood movie.*

"If you stay in front of the movie camera long enough, it will show you not only what you had for breakfast, but also who your ancestors were."

> — *John Barrymore*

"It's a great profession, so long as nobody ever catches you at it."

> — *Spencer Tracy, on acting*

"When Nijinsky visited Chaplin on a set, Charlie was about to have a custard pie in his face, and Nijinsky said, `The nuances! The miraculous timing!' And it's a lot of bunk. You laugh, you cry, you pick up a little bit, and then you're a working actor . . . Life's what's important: Walking, houses, family. Birth and pain and joy. And then death. Acting's just waiting for a custard pie. That's all."

> — *Katharine Hepburn*

"I'm a sensitive writer, actor, and director. Talking business disgusts me. If you want to do business, call my disgusting personal manager."
— *Sylvester Stallone, the sensitive star who earns over $20 million per movie*

"If I had my life to live over I would do everything the exact same way — with the possible exception of seeing the movie remake of *Lost Horizon*."
— *Woody Allen*

"Any girl can be glamourous. All you have to do is stand still and look stupid."
— *Hedy Lamarr*

"That's the trouble, a sex symbol becomes a thing. I just hate being a thing."
— *Marilyn Monroe*

"In Europe an actor is an artist. In Hollywood, if he isn't working, he's a bum."
— *Anthony Quinn*

"I was out there eight months. I worked five weeks and got three years' pay."
— *Fanny Brice on Hollywood*

"A celebrity is one who works all his life to become well-known and then goes through back streets wearing dark glasses so he won't be recognized."

— *Jane Powell*

"Part of the loot went for gambling, and part for women. The rest I spent foolishly."
    — *George Raft, on how he spent $10 million over the course of his career*

"There is only one thing that can kill the movies and that is education."

— *Will Rogers*

"All Americans born between 1890 and 1945 wanted to be movie stars."

— *Gore Vidal*

THE CRITICS SPEAK OUT

"Good movies make you care, make you believe in possibilities again."

— *Pauline Kael*

"The lowest action trash is preferable to whole-some family entertainment. When you clean them up, when you make movies respectable, you kill them."

— *Pauline Kael*

"We are drawn to our television sets each April the way we are drawn to the scene of an accident."

— *Vincent Canby on the Academy Awards*

FAMOUS LAST WORDS

"Young man, you can be grateful that my invention is not for sale, for it would un-doubtedly ruin you. It can be exploited for a certain time as a scientific curiosity, but apart from that it has no commercial value whatso-ever."

— *Auguste Lumiere, co-inventor of modern cinematography, 1895*

ON HOLLYWOOD

"It's a mining town in lotus land."

— *F. Scott Fitzgerald*

"Hollywood is a place where they'll pay you $50,000 for a kiss and 50 cents for your soul."

— *Marilyn Monroe*

"You can take all the sincerity in Hollywood, place it in the navel of a fruit fly and still have room enough for three caraway seeds and a producer's heart."

— *Fred Allen*

"It's a great place to live, but I wouldn't want to visit there."

— *Will Rogers*

"When it's 100 degrees in New York, it's 72 in Los Angeles. When it's 30 degrees in New York, in Los Angeles it's still 72. However, there are 6 million interesting people in New York, and 72 in Los Angeles."

— *Neil Simon*

"The convictions of Hollywood and television are made of boiled money."

— *Lillian Hellman*

"Hollywood stinks."

— *Frank Sinatra*

"Hollywood always had a streak of the totalitarian in just about everything it did."
— *Shirley MacLaine*

"Hollywood's queens and kings lived far more luxuriously than most of the reigning families in Europe. Most of them tossed their money around as though they manufactured it themselves in the cellar. They went in for solid gold bathtubs, chauffeur-driven Rolls Royces, champagne for breakfast and caviar every fifteen minutes. It was the kind of world that today only exists in the pages of movie magazines and for the sons of a few Latin American dictators."
— *Groucho Marx*

"It's somehow symbolic of Hollywood that Tara was just a facade, with no rooms inside."
— *David O Selznick*

"It's a great place to live . . . if you're an orange."
— *Fred Allen*

"Hollywood may be thickly populated, but to me it's still a bewilderness."
— *Sir Cedrick Hardwicke*

"In Hollywood, if you didn't sing or dance you would end up as an after-dinner speaker, so they made me an after-dinner speaker."
— *Ronald Reagan*

"Hollywood is not uncivilized, it is decivilized."
— *Writer Patrick Mahoney*

"No man could find a better spot on earth, if only he had an intelligent person to talk to."
— *Aldous Huxley*

"Hollywood is where they shoot too many pictures and not enough actors."
— *Walter Winchell*

"Hollywood is a place where if you don't find happiness you send out for it."
— *Rex Reed*

"Hollywood is a place where the stars twinkle until they wrinkle."
— *Victor Mature*

"Hollywood is a place where they have great respect for the dead, but none for the living."
— *Errol Flynn*

"A Hollywood starlet is the name given to any woman under thirty not actively employed in a brothel."

— Ben Hecht

"Hollywood is divided into two classes — those who own swimming pools and those who can't keep their heads above water."

— Jimmy Durante

"Hollywood is where they mix a beautiful doll with a few feet of Technicolor — and wind up with a beautiful dollar."

— Jack Benny

"Hollywood is a place where you often find a combination of hot heads and cold shoulders."

— Gregory Peck

"Hollywood is a place where a man can get stabbed in the back while climbing a ladder."

— William Faulkner

"In Hollywood success is relative. The closer the relative, the greater the success."

— actor Arthur Treacher

"Hollywood is the only town where you can say, 'Come up and see me some time,' and not get taken up on it."

— *Mae West*

"I've had a wonderful evening, but this wasn't it!"

— *Groucho Marx to the hostess of a Hollywood party he was leaving*

"They have found that mutual hatred is not sufficient basis for a successful marriage. There has to be a little more."

— *Ben Hecht, on the divorce of a Hollywood couple*

"There's a good reason why so many Hollywood girls get married in the morning: They want the afternoon free to plan their divorces."

— *Cornel Wilde*

THE WIT & WISDOM OF PRODUCERS

"When he arrives in his office in the morning, there's a molehill on his desk, and by nightfall he has to make a mountain out of it."

— *Fred Allen on the assistant producer*

"Directors have to be on the set all the time, and the one thing I've noticed as an actor in fifty-two pictures is that every time it starts to rain the producer goes back to the hotel and you all sit there and get soaked. And he also has more Monets and Picassos on his wall; and he always has a bigger house than everybody. In Hollywood anyway. I noticed that very early on, and I thought, that's what I want to be. I want all the paintings; I want to be back in the hotel when it's raining."

— *Michael Caine, explaining why he'd rather be a producer than a director*

"Executives here will tell you they don't like yes-men. But there are very few no-men working."

— *producer Mark Hellinger to up-and-coming producer Fred de Cordova*

"Don't say yes until I'm finished talking!"
— *Darryl Zanuck*

"A producer is a man who asks you a question, gives you the answer, and then tells you what's wrong with it."

— *producer Lamarr Trotti*

"You call this a script? Give me a couple of $5,000-a-week writers and I'll write it myself!"

> — *Hungarian producer Joe Pasternak*

"Why let two thousand years of publicity go to waste?"

> — *Cecil B. DeMille,*
> *explaining why he was going to remake*
> *The Ten Commandments (1956)*

"If I knew I was going to live this long, I'd have taken better care of myself."

> — *movie mogul Adolph Zukor,*
> *on his 100th birthday*

"I gave up smoking two years ago."

> — *Adolph Zukor, 103,*
> *on the secret of his long life*

"I wouldn't pay $50,000 for any damn book, any time."

> — *Jack Warner, while turning down the*
> *opportunity to film Gone With the Wind*

"Who the hell wants to hear actors talk?"

> — *Harry Warner, on his brothers' plans*
> *to make sound films*

"If there's anything I can't stand, it's yes-men. When I say no, I want you to say no too."
— *Jack Warner to a publicist*

"I love Mickey Mouse more than any woman I've ever known."
— *Walt Disney*

"Novelty is always welcome, but talking pictures are just a fad."
— *Irving Thalberg, after the premier of the first feature sound film, The Jazz Singer (1927)*

REAGAN IN HOLLYWOOD

"It's our fault. We should have given him better parts."
— *Jack Warner on hearing that Ronald Reagan had been elected Governor of California*

"I think he was in Hollywood too long. He signed it, `Best wishes, Ronald Reagan.'"
— *Johnny Carson, after Reagan had signed a new tax law*

THE MUCH-MALIGNED WRITER

"Hi boy! What you spoilin' now?"
— *Will Rogers method of greeting screenwriters*

"The Number One Book of the Ages was written by a committee. It's called the Bible."
— *Louis B. Mayer responding to a screenwriter's complaints about changes made to his script*

"This is a terrific script. It just needs a complete rewrite."
— *director Peter Bogdanovich to Alvin Sargent after reading his screenplay for Paper Moon (1973)*

"I don't want to be right; I just want to keep working."
— *screenwriter Arthur Caesar*

"When in doubt, have two guys come through the door with guns."
— *Raymond Chandler*

It's a fine motion picture up to the point where God finishes and the script writer takes over."

— *Will Rogers on The Ten Commandments (1923).*

"In Hollywood, the woods are full of people that learned to write, but evidently can't read. If they could read their stuff, they'd stop writing."

— *Will Rogers on screenwriters*

"Nothing puts me to sleep faster than the sound of my collaborator's typewriter."

— *screenwriter Herman Mankiewicz*

"I didn't last long. I went out [to Hollywood] for a thousand a week, and I worked Monday, and I got fired Wednesday. The guy that hired me was out of town Tuesday."

— *Nelson Algren*

MASTERS OF THE MALAPROP: SAMUEL GOLDWYN AND MIKE CURTIZ

GOLDWYNISMS

The legendary film producer and movie mogul Samuel Goldwyn was known for his hilarious abuses of the English language.

"Our comedies are not to be laughed at."

"I've been laid up with intentional flu."

"I love the ground I walk on."

"For this part I want a lady, somebody that's couth."

"You need Indians? You can get them right from the reservoir."

"I'll write you a blanket check."

"I don't think anybody should write his autobiography until after he's dead."

"I want to make a picture about the Russian secret police: the GOP."

"I can answer you in two words — im possible."

"We've passed a lot of water since then."

"I would be sticking my head in a moose."

"I ran into George Kaufman the other night. He was at my house for dinner."

"I can't make it, but I hope you'll give me a raincoat."
                          — *after being invited to dinner*

"A verbal contract isn't worth the paper it's written on."

"That's the trouble with directors. Always biting the hand that lays the golden egg."

"Anybody who goes to see a psychiatrist ought to have his head examined."

"Include me out."

"I want to go where the hand of man has never set foot."

"Gentlemen, do not underestimate the danger of the atom bomb. It's dynamite!"

"Even if they had it in the streets, I wouldn't go."

— said while explaining why he didn't want to attend Mardi Gras in New Orleans

"You are partly one hundred percent right."

"I'm going out for some tea and trumpets."

"Go ahead, but make copies of them first."

— after a secretary asked him if she could destroy some old files

"It will create an excitement that will sweep the country like wildflowers."

"Go ahead, make a bust of them."

— after a sculptor commented on the beauty of Mrs. Goldwyn's hands

"I don't care if it don't make a nickel, so long as everyone in the United States sees it."

— after The Best Years of Our Lives (1946) took the Oscar for best film

"He's living beyond his means, but he can afford it."

"No, I would rather deal with a smart idiot than with a stupid genius."
> — *turning down a director known for his huge artistic ego*

"A wide screen just makes a bad film twice as bad."

"Why only twelve? Go out and get thousands!"
> — *on re-staging the Last Supper*

"I read part of it all the way through."

"It always makes me very unhappy to say good-bye to a clog in my machine." — *to an employee who was leaving the studio*

MIKE CURTIZ

This Hungarian-born director of Casablanca (1942) is also known for his bizarre sayings.

"Don't talk to me while I'm interrupting."
"Now ride off in all directions."
> — *to Gary Cooper, who was sitting on a horse, waiting for the action to begin*

"Keep quiet, you're always interrupting me in the middle of my mistakes."

"I want this house over-furnished in perfect taste."

"The next time I send a dope, I'll go myself."
> — *to a production assistant*
> *who brought back the wrong prop*

"It's dull from beginning to end . . . But it's loaded with entertainment."
> — *when asked his opinion on a film*

"I'm very sorry, but I ran like a fire hydrant."
> — *excusing himself for being late*

"I got a phone call from Jack Warner at one in the morning. He pulled me out of bed. It's a lucky thing I was playing gin rummy."

"It's just fine. I gave them two choices: take it or leave it."
> — *about a contract negotiation*

IT'S ALL IN THE NAME

Cecil B. DeMille's middle name is Blount.

David O. Selznick doesn't really have a middle name. He thought that the O would make his name a bit more classy.

Dean Martin's real name is Dino Crocetti.

Mickey Rooney's real name is Joe Yule Jr.

Rudolph Valentino's real name was Rodolfo Alfonzo Raffaelo Pierre Filibert Guglielmi di Valentina d'Antonguolla.

Scrappy, Hoppy, Awful, Crabby, Daffy, Busy, Helpful, Snoopy, Thrifty, Flabby, and Dumpy were among the names considered for the dwarfs in *Snow White and the Seven Dwarfs*.

Harry Houdini gave the name "Buster" to Buster Keaton.

Cary Grant's real name is Archibald Alexander Leach.

Jerry Lewis' real name is Joseph Levitch.

Jane Wyman's real name is Sarah Jane Fulks.

Edward G. Robinson's real name was Emanuel Goldenberg.

Dirk Bogard's real name was Derek Julius Gaspard Ulrich Niven van den Bogaerde.

Walter Matthau's real name is Walter Matuschanskayasky.

Sandra Dee's real name is Alexandra Zuck.

Doris Day's real name is Doris Kappelhoff.

Burl Ives' real name is Burl Ivanhoe.

Rita Hayworth's real name was Margarita Carmen Cansino.

Anne Bancroft's real name is Anna Maria Luisa Italiano.

Tony Curtis' real name is Bernard Schwarz.

Bob Hope's real name is Leslie Hope.

Bing Crosby's real name was Harry Crosby.

Groucho Marx's real name was Julius Marx.

Zsa Zsa Gabor's real name is Sari Gabor.

Joan Crawford's real name was Lucille Le Sueur.

Bela Lugosi's real name was Bela Blasko.

Carole Lombard's real name was Jane Peters.

Samuel Goldwyn's real name was Samuel Goldfish.

Kirk Douglas' real name is Issur Danielovitch.

Cyd Charisse was born Tula Ellice Finklea. Her brother nicknamed her Sid. During a stint with the ballet, she changed her name to Felicia Sidarova, which she later changed to Maria Estamano. After a marriage, she became Nico Charisse. Early on in her movie career she was known as Lily Norwood. MGM changed this to Sid Charisse, and ultimately to Cyd Charisse.

TOP TENS AND OTHER LISTS

THE TOP TEN FILM
PRODUCING COUNTRIES
(Average Number of Films Produced Per Year)

1) India (810)
2) Japan (309)
3) USA (257)
4) Taiwan (186)
5) Philippines (160)
6) USSR (155)
7) France (152)
8) Turkey (150)
9) Hong Kong (136)
10) Thailand (130)

THE TOP TEN SPORTS IN MOVIES

1) Boxing
2) Horse Racing
3) Football
4) Auto Racing
5) Baseball
6) Track and Field
7) Basketball
8) Wrestling
9) Golf
10) Motorcycle Racing

THE TOP 25 GROSSING FILMS OF ALL TIME

1) *E.T. The Extra-Terrestrial* (1982)
2) *Star Wars* (1977)
3) *Return of the Jedi* (1983)
4) *Batman* (1989)
5) *The Empire Strikes Back* (1980)
6) *Ghostbusters* (1984)
7) *Home Alone* (1990)
8) *Jaws* (1975)
9) *Raiders of the Lost Ark* (1981)
10) *Indiana Jones and the Last Crusade* (1989)
11) *Indiana Jones and the Temple of Doom* (1984)
12) *Beverly Hills Cop* (1984)
13) *Back to the Future* (1985)
14) *Grease* (1978)
15) *Tootsie* (1982)
16) *Ghost* (1990)
17) *The Exorcist* (1973)
18) *Rain Man* (1988)
19) *The Godfather* (1972)
20) *Superman* (1978)
21) *Close Encounters of the Third Kind* (1977)
22) *Pretty Woman* (1990)
23) *Three Men and a Baby* (1987)
24) *Who Framed Roger Rabbit* (1988)
25) *Beverly Hills Cop II* (1987)

THE MOST POPULAR HORROR FILMS
(From 1970 to 1990)

1970 — *House of Dark Shadows*
1971 — *Willard*
1972 — *Frenzy*
1973 — *Legend of Hell House*
1974 — *The Exorcist*
1975 — *Jaws*
1976 — *The Omen*
1977 — *King Kong*
1978 — *Jaws II*
1979 — *Alien/Amityville Horror*
1980 — *The Shining*
1981 — *An American Werewolf in London*
1982 — *Poltergeist*
1983 — *Jaws 3-D*
1984 — *Gremlins*
1985 — *Teen Wolf*
1986 — *Aliens*
1987 — *Witches of Eastwick/Predator*
1988 — *A Nightmare on Elm Street 4*
1989 — *Pet Cemetery*
1990 — *Arachnophobia*

THE MOST POPULAR MALE AND FEMALE STARS
(From 1970 to 1990)

1970 — Paul Newman, Barbra Streisand
1971 — John Wayne, Ali McGraw
1972 — Clint Eastwood, Barbra Streisand
1973 — Clint Eastwood, Barbra Streisand
1974 — Robert Redford, Barbra Streisand
1975 — Robert Redford, Barbra Streisand
1976 — Robert Redford, Tatum O'Neal
1977 — Sylvester Stallone, Barbra Streisand
1978 — Burt Reynolds, Diane Keaton
1979 — Burt Reynolds, Jane Fonda
1980 — Burt Reynolds, Jane Fonda
1981 — Burt Reynolds, Dolly Parton
1982 — Burt Reynolds, Dolly Parton
1983 — Clint Eastwood, Meryl Streep
1984 — Clint Eastwood, Sally Field
1985 — Sylvester Stallone, Meryl Streep
1986 — Tom Cruise, Bette Midler
1987 — Eddie Murphy, Glenn Close
1988 — Tom Cruise, Bette Midler
1989 — Jack Nicholson, Kathleen Turner
1990 — Arnold Schwarznegger, Julia Roberts

THE FIVE LONGEST FILM TITLES

1) *The Persecution and Assassination of Jean-Paul Marat as Performed by the Inmates of the Asylum of Charenton Under the Direction of the Marquis de Sade* (1966).

2) *Why Do I Believe You When You Tell Me That You Love Me, When I Know You've Been a Liar All Your Life?* (1983)

3) *Those Magnificent Men in Their Flying Machines: or, How I Flew from London to Paris in 25 Hours and 11 Minutes* (1965).

4) *Cafeteria or How Are You Going to Keep Her Down on the Farm After She's Seen Paris Twice?* (1973).

5) *The Saga of the Viking Women and Their Voyage to the Waters of the Great Sea Serpent* (1957).

TEN STRANGE MOVIE TITLES

1) $ (1972)
2) **** (1967)
3) *Who's the Fattest Fish of All?* (1969)
4) *Phffft* (1954)
5) *In My Time Boys Didn't Use Hair Cream* (1937)
6) *I Know That You Know I Know* (1982)
7) *Beautiful Lady Without Neck* (1966)
8) *Don't Worry, We'll Think of a Title* (1965)
9) *Recharge Grandmothers Exactly!* (1984)
10) *The Film That Rises to the Surface of Clarified Butter* (1968)

OSCAR WINNERS FOR BEST FILM OF THE YEAR

1929 — *Wings*
1930 (March) — *Broadway Melody*
1930 (Nov) — *All Quiet on the Western Front*
1931 — *Cimarron*
1932 — *Grand Hotel*
1933 — No Academy Awards Ceremony
1934 — *Cavalcade*
1935 — *It Happened One Night*
1936 — *Mutiny on the Bounty*

1937 — *The Great Ziegfeld*
1938 — *The Life of Emile Zola*
1939 — *You Can't Take It With You*
1940 — *Gone With the Wind*
1941 — *Rebecca*
1942 — *How Green Was My Valley*
1943 — *Mrs Miniver*
1944 — *Casablanca*
1945 — *Going My Way*
1946 — *The Lost Weekend*
1947 — *The Best Years of Our Lives*
1948 — *Gentlemen's Agreement*
1949 — *Hamlet*
1950 — *All the King's Men*
1951 — *All About Eve*
1952 — *An American in Paris*
1953 — *The Greatest Show On Earth*
1954 — *From Here To Eternity*
1955 — *On The Waterfront*
1956 — *Marty*
1957 — *Around the World in 80 Days*
1958 — *The Bridge on the River Kwai*
1959 — *Gigi*
1960 — *Ben Hur*
1961 — *The Apartment*
1962 — *West Side Story*
1963 — *Lawrence of Arabia*
1964 — *Tom Jones*

1965 — *My Fair Lady*
1966 — *The Sound of Music*
1967 — *A Man for All Seasons*
1968 — *In the Heat of the Night*
1969 — *Oliver!*
1970 — *Midnight Cowboy*
1971 — *Patton*
1972 — *The French Connection*
1973 — *The Godfather*
1974 — *The Sting*
1975 — *The Godfather, Part II*
1976 — *One Flew Over the Cuckoo's Nest*
1977 — *Rocky*
1978 — *Annie Hall*
1979 — *The Deer Hunter*
1980 — *Kramer vs Kramer*
1981 — *Ordinary People*
1982 — *Chariots of Fire*
1983 — *Ghandi*
1984 — *Terms of Endearment*
1985 — *Amadeus*
1986 — *Out of Africa*
1987 — *Platoon*
1988 — *The Last Emperor*
1989 — *Rain Man*
1990 — *Driving Miss Daisy*
1991 — *Dances With Wolves*
1992 — *The Silence of the Lambs*

FIFTY FACTS ABOUT ELEVEN HOLLYWOOD SUPERSTARS

HUMPHREY BOGART

1) Despite the fact that he had appeared on Broadway with Leslie Howard in *The Peterified Forest*, Bogart was not wanted for the 1936 film version of the play. The studio preferred Edward G. Robinson, but Leslie Howard insisted that Bogart get the role or else he was off the project himself. To honor Howard, Bogart named his daughter Leslie.

2) Bogart could be found eating lunch at Romanoff's in Beverly Hills virtually every day when he wasn't working.

3) After he failed at his first attempt to crack Hollywood, Bogart returned to New York and performed in the theater. He supported himself between gigs by playing chess for one dollar a game at a Manhattan arcade.

4) Bogart played Dr. Maurice Xavier in the only horror film of his career, *The Return of Dr. X* (1939).

MARLON BRANDO

5) Brando dated Rita Moreno in the late '50s.

6) Comedian Wally Cox was Brando's best friend for years until his death in 1973.

7) Brando received $2.5 million for his portrayal of Jar-El, Superman's father from Krypton, in the film *Superman* (1978).

8) Brando was born in Omaha, Nebraska.

9) Brando was told to pick a local Tahitian beauty to play Maimiti, Fletcher Christian's concubine in *Mutiny on the Bounty* (1962). He chose Tarita Teriipaia, who would later give birth to their son.

JOAN CRAWFORD

10) In 1968, when Crawford's daughter, Christina, could not make her regular appearance in the soap opera, "The Secret Storm," due to an illness, Crawford filled in for her.

11) After Crawford married Douglas Fairbanks, Jr., her in-laws — Douglas Fairbanks and Mary Pickford — refused to meet her for some eight months. They evidently thought their son deserved better.

12) Crawford won the Oscar for her comeback performance in *Mildred Pierce* (1945). She had not made a film in two years.

13) It is rumored that Crawford had affairs with Spencer Tracy, Clark Gable, Glenn Ford, and William Paley.

BETTE DAVIS

14) When Davis appeared in a scene in *Old Acquaintance* (1943) wearing a man's pajama top as a nightgown, she created a new fashion sensation — the shorty nightgown.

15) Davis once told comedian Jonathan Winters to "go to hell" while they were on the Jack Paar show. Winters had just done an imitation of the actress.

16) Davis' famous line, "What a dump," was actually from one of her worst reviewed films — *Beyond the Forest* (1949).

CLARK GABLE

17) 13-year-old Judy Garland sang "You Made Me Love You" at Gable's 36th birthday party.

18) Gable's first two wives — Josephine Dillion and Ria Langhan — were 14 and 17 years older than the star respectively.

19) In the summer of 1942, Gable enlisted in the army in honor of his late wife Carole Lombard. She had been killed in a plane crash while on a tour selling war bonds.

20) Gable's real name was William Clark Gable.

21) When Gable was first cast in *It Happened One Night* (1934), he told director Frank Capra that he would give the role a shot, but if things weren't going well after a few days he would leave the production.

CARY GRANT

22) Grant never won an Academy Award, although he did receive an honorary Oscar in 1970.

23) Grant proposed to Sophia Loren in 1957 while they were filming *The Pride and the Passion*. She turned him down.

24) In 1922 Grant walked on stilts in costume at Coney Island.

25) A magazine once sent a telegram to Grant, asking, "How old Cary Grant?" Grant's reply was, "Old Cary fine, how you?"

26) Mae West, while casting *She Done Him Wrong* (1933), said of Grant, "If this one can talk, I'll take him."

KATHARINE HEPBURN

27) After Hepburn appeared on "The Dick Cavett Show" in 1973 — her first televised interview — she was bombarded by offers of work.

28) Hepburn was married one time in her life — to Ludlow Ogden Smith in 1928. The marriage lasted all of three weeks.

29) Hepburn and Spencer Tracy were romantically, and secretly, involved for many, many years.

30) Dorothy Parker, reviewing a flawed Broadway play, *The Lake* (1933), said of Hepburn's performance, "She ran the gamut of emotions from A to B."

31) Hepburn was self-conscious of her long neck, which she often covered with scarves and high collars. In films, small spotlights are often used to hide this unusual feature.

MARILYN MONROE

32) Monroe and husband/playwright Arthur Miller worked on one film together — *The Misfits* (1961). Not only did it turn out to be Monroe's last film, but it was also the final appearance of co-star Clark Gable.

33) At 23, Monroe had surgery on her jaw and had the tip of her nose bobbed.

34) Monroe has been romantically linked with Frank Sinatra, Marlon Brando, Yves Montand, and Harry Cohn, among others.

35) Joe Dimaggio was so outraged when he watched the filming of then-wife Monroe's legendary scene in *The Seven Year Itch* (1955) — in which the actress' skirt blows up as she stands over a subway grating — that he divorced her within two weeks.

36) Monroe appeared on stage at Madison Square Garden in 1962 to sing "Happy Birthday" to President Kennedy.

JIMMY STEWART

37) When Stewart was a young man, his favorite instrument was the accordian.

38) Stewart won an Academy Award for best actor in *The Philadelphia Story* (1940), and was nominated for his performances in four others: *Mr. Smith Goes to Washington* (1939), *It's a Wonderful Life* (1946), *Harvey* (1950), and *Anatomy of a Murder* (1959).

39) Long considered the most eligible bachelor in Hollywood — he didn't marry until he was 41 — Stewart dated Ginger Rogers, Jean Harlow, Marlene Dietrich, and Lana Turner, among others.

40) Stewart was awarded the Distinguished Flying Cross for leading his bomber squadron on a dangerous mission over Germany.

41) Stewart once shared a flat with Henry Fonda while the two of them were struggling actors.

42) Stewart was elected to the Cowboy Hall of Fame in 1972. He starred in 18 westerns.

ELIZABETH TAYLOR

43) Taylor almost didn't land the role of Velvet Brown in *National Velvet* (1944) because the producer considered her to be too short for the role. He eventually decided to postpone production for a few months to allow the actress to grow.

44) One of Taylor's closest friends was fellow-actor Montgomery Clift, whom she met while filming *A Place in the Sun* (1951).

45) Taylor's first appearance in a Broadway play was in a 1981 revival of Lillian Hellman's *The Little Foxes*.

46) Taylor's first serious relationship was with football hero Glenn Davis. She broke off their engagement when she met millionaire Bill Pawley.

JOHN WAYNE

47) Wayne's first starring role was in *The Big Trail* (1929), and his first huge commercial success was in *Stagecoach* (1939).

48) After being turned down by the United States Naval Academy, Wayne accepted a scholarship from the University of Southern California.

49) Wayne died of lung cancer in 1979 — he was known to smoke five packs of unfiltered cigarettes a day.

50) When Wayne was a child, he would go to the movies five times a week. His father owned a pharmacy that was housed in the same building as a movie theater, the owner of which let young John in for free.

TEST YOUR MOVIE TRIVIA KNOWLEDGE

ACTORS
(Answers begin on page 118)

1) Who was Greta Garbo's leading man in the '20s?

2) Who is the oldest actor to win an Academy Award?

3) Who was originally cast to play the role that eventually went to Marlon Brando in *On the Waterfront*?

4) Who won an Academy Award for his performance as Maggio in *From Here to Eternity*?

5) These two actors starred as drifters in the film *Scarecrow*.

6) He played Jeremiah Johnson in the film of the same name.

7) Who played the choreographer in *All That Jazz*?

8) Who played the two male lead roles in *Bob and Carol and Ted and Alice*?

9) Who made Greta Garbo laugh in *Ninotchka*?

10) Who invited his friends on a cruise to discover who murdered his wife in *The Last of Shiela*?

11) Included among his films are *A Raisin In the Sun*, *Porgy and Bess*, and *To Sir With Love*.

12) Strong and silent, he won fans in such films as *Bullitt* and *The Great Escape*.

13) While now known for his role in American Express commercials and for his portrayal of a detective in a popular television show, this actor once received an Academy Award nomination for his performance in Tennessee Williams' *A Streetcar Named Desire*.

14) A major box office star, this actor has appeared in such varied films as *The Fortune Cookie*, *The Sunshine Boys*, and *Hopscotch*.

15) This popular French singer had success in Hollywood with *On A Clear Day You Can See Forever*, *The Wages of Fear*, and *Z*.

16) Who played the Scottish private in *King of Hearts*?

17) He fell in love with older woman Lily Tomlin in *Moment by Moment*.

18) He won an Academy Award for his performance as Sir Thomas More in *A Man For All Seasons*.

19) Who won the Academy Award for playing a corrupt chief of police in *In the Heat of the Night*?

20) He played a male hustler in *Midnight Cowboy*.

- 21) Who made his film debut in Hitchcock's *The Lady Vanishes*?

22) Goldie Hawn fell in love with his character in *Butterflies are Free*.

23) Who forced his men to build *The Bridge Over River Kwai*?

24) He falls for Audrey Hepburn in *Breakfast at Tiffany's*.

25) Who played Woody Guthrie in *Bound for Glory*?

26) Knighted in 1947, this great actor starred in such films as *Richard III*, *The Looking Glass War*, and *Things to Come*.

27) One of the most gifted actors and singers in the history of cinema, this man starred in such films as *Showboat*, *The Emperor Jones*, and *Tales of Manhattan*.

28) He won an Academy Award for his performance in *Judgment at Nuremberg*.

29) Who co-starred with Diana Ross in *Lady Sings the Blues*?

30) What two British comics teamed up in *The Ladykillers*?

31) He's played villians and/or cowboys in everything from *Shane* to *The Big Knife* to *City Slickers*.

32) This great film maker also starred in such films as *Rosemary's Baby* and *The Dirty Dozen*.

33) He made a stunning cameo as a Jew mutilated by a Nazi in *Judgment at Nuremberg*.

34) As a child, he was featured in *Oliver Twist* and *The Kid*.

35) This strong and silent star appeared in *Sergeant York* and *The Fountainhead*.

36) Primarily known as a writer and composer, this remarkable talent starred in *Our Man In Havana* and *The Scoundrel*.

37) Who co-starred with Susan Sarandon in Louis Malle's *Atlantic City*?

38) Film's funniest duo, they starred in *Big Business* and *The Battle of the Century* among many others.

39) While many remember him for his portrayal of Frankenstein, this actor also appeared in *The Body Snatchers* and *Isle of the Dead*.

40) One of the great silent film comedians, he made his final screen appearance in *A Funny Thing Happened On the Way to the Forum*.

41) He rocked Hollywood when he teamed up with Peter Fonda in *Easy Rider*.

42) One of the biggest stars of the '60s, he starred in *Pillow Talk* and *Man's Favorite Sport*.

43) He starred with Mae West in *She Done Him Wrong* before going on to such films as *North By Northwest* and *The Philadelphia Story*.

44) Who played eight different roles in *Kind Hearts and Coronets*?

45) Who co-starred with Elizabeth Taylor in *The Taming of the Shrew*?

46) The only actor recognized because of his bald head, he starred in such classics as *The Ten Commandments*, *The Magnificent Seven*, and *The King and I*.

47) He starred in *Spartacus*, *Gunfight at the OK Corral*, and *Seven Days in May*.

48) A huge star of the '70s and '80s, he made his name in the spaghetti western *A Fistful of Dollars*.

49) He won an Academy Award for his performance in his last film, *Network*.

50) This remarkable actor's career stretches from *The Grapes of Wrath* to *Mr. Roberts* to *On Golden Pond*.

51) He made his first appearance in 1931's *The Painted Desert* and his last in 1960's *The Misfits*.

52) He first became a star with his performance as a child molester in Fritz Lang's *M*.

53) A tough guy in most of his films, one of his best loved is *Yankee Doodle Dandy*.

54) Who played the paralyzed war veteran in *The Men*?

55) Who played the comic who ends up involved with some gangsters in *Mickey One*?

56) This actor played a gambler who organizes a war drive bazaar to raise money for a game in the film *Mr. Lucky*.

57) Who played Casanova in Fellini's film of the same name?

58) This man with the straw hat can be seen in the musicals *Gigi* and *Folies Bergere*.

59) He is known for his roles in *White Christmas* and *The Inspector General*.

60) This contemporary actor has starred in *Jaws*, *The Apprenticeship of Duddy Kravitz*, and *The Good-bye Girl*.

61) He danced throughout *An American In Paris*.

62) Who co-starred with Gene Kelly in *Singing in the Rain*?

63) He played a rock star in Nicholas Roeg's *Performance*.

64) Who is Shirley MacLaine's brother?

65) He was cast as a female impersonator in his first film, but later went on to play tough guys in such movies as *The Champ* and *Barnacle Bill*.

66) Who are the two co-stars of *Citizen Kane*?

67) He starred in *The Hospital* and *Rage*, but is best known for his role as Patton.

ACTRESSES
(*Answers begin on page 120*)

1) Who played the two sisters in *Psycho*?

2) Who played Delilah to Victor Mature's Samson in *Samson and Delilah*?

3) She won an Academy Award for her performance as Alma in *From Here to Eternity*. -

4) She was the first black actress to ever win an Academy Award.

5) She was the object of John Wayne's search in *The Searchers*.

6) Who played the hooker with the heart of gold in *Sweet Charity*?

7) What actress co-starred with Laurence Olivier in *The Prince and the Showgirl*?

8) What actress, a great performer in her own right, was married to John Cassavetes, and starred in his film *A Woman Under the Influence*?

9) Who played Sally Bowles in *Cabaret*?

10) Who played opposite Jimmy Stewart in *The Man Who Knew Too Much*?

11) She was *The Lady From Shanghai*.

12) Which two sex symbols co-starred in *Gentlemen Prefer Blondes*.

13) Who played the title role in *Irma La Douce*?

14) She played Fanny Brice in the musical *Funny Girl*.

15) She was the star of the 70s' film, *An Unmarried Woman*.

16) She chased Ryan O'Neal in *Paper Moon*.

17) Who played the librarian Marion in *The Music Man*?.

18) These two actresses played Mary Astor's children in *Meet Me in St. Louis*.

19) Who played Orson Welles' mistress in *The Long, Hot Summer*?.

20) This actress played Sylvester Stallone's shy girlfriend in *Rocky*.

21) She co-starred with Marlon Brando in *Reflections in a Golden Eye*.

22) Who fell in love with Warren Beatty in *Splendor in the Grass*?

23) What Academy Award nominee played Pookie Adams in *The Sterile Cuckoo*?

24) What actress played Siamese twins in Brian De Palma's *Sisters*?

25) In *Sounder*, her sharecropper husband was sent to prison.

26) Who was known as America's tap-dancing sweetheart?

27) What two actresses starred as Helen Keller and Annie Sullivan in *The Miracle Worker*?

28) Who co-starred with Humphrey Bogart in *The Barefoot Contessa*?

29) She was a young starlet succumbing to the pressures of stardom in *Valley of the Dolls*.

30) Which actress was the first to demand and receive $1 million for a role?

31) She played the "mousey" wife in *Who's Afraid of Virginia Woolf*.

32) She played Katharine Ross' best friend in *The Stepford Wives*.

33) This actress tried to steal Spencer Tracy away from Katharine Hepburn in *State of the Union*.

34) Who played the eerie neighbor in *Rosemary's Baby*?

35) She played the French actress in *The Last Tycoon*.

36) Who co-starred with Gregory Peck in *Spellbound*?

37) Two other actresses besides Elizabeth Taylor are known for their performance as Cleopatra. Who are they?

38) She played the gorgeous mistress in *Room at the Top*.

39) These two great entertainers appeared with Nat "King" Cole in *St. Louis Blues*.

40) She co-starred with Woody Allen in
Sleeper.

41) Who played Iris, the twelve year old
prostitute, in *Taxi Driver*?

42) She played the beautiful, neurotic
actress in Woody Allen's *Stardust Memories*.

43) Who played the female sidekick to Bob
Hope and Bing Crosby in their famous road
pictures?

44) She was Laurence Olivier's second wife
in *Rebecca*.

45) Who co-starred with Bette Davis in
Hush, Hush Sweet Charlotte?

46) Who played opposite Clark Gable in *It
Happened One Night*?

47) Who co-starred with Fred Astaire in
Funny Face?

48) Name the youngest actress to ever
appear on the cover of *Time* magazine.

49) What actress was the first centerfold for *Playboy* magazine?

50) Who played the title role in *Alice Doesn't Live Here Anymore*?

51) Who played the sloppy housekeeper in *Hush, Hush Sweet Charlotte*?

52) She won Academy Awards for her performances in *The Diary of Anne Frank* and *A Patch of Blue*.

MOVIES
(*Answers begin on page 122*)

1) *Star Wars* was the highest grossing film of 1977. What was the second highest?

2) What was the only sequel to ever win the Best Picture Oscar?

3) It was Frankie Avalon and Annette Funicello's first beach-party movie.

4) This comedy-western is Mel Brooks' most famous and popular film.

5) Spencer Tracy and Katharine Hepburn's on-screen daughter falls in love with Sidney Portier in this film.

6) Elizabeth Taylor, Paul Newman, and Burl Ives starred in this version of Tennessee Williams' classic play.

7) Alan Arkin starred in this version of Joseph Heller's absurd novel about war.

8) Richard Roundtree played this detective in the film of the same name.

9) Clark Gable and Burt Lancaster starred in this story of submarine warfare.

10) Ernest Borgnine won an Academy Award for his touching performance in this film, which takes its title from Borgnine's character.

11) What film features Jon Voight and Dustin Hoffman as hustlers?

12) David Bowie stars in this science fiction movie.

13) In this 8th James Bond film, Roger Moore tries to break up a heroin smuggling ring.

14) Woody Allen and Diane Keaton star in this parody of Russian novels.

15) What Alfred Hitchcock film climaxes inside the Statue of Liberty?

16) What love story featured Audrey Hepburn and Sean Connery?

17) Gregory Peck falls in love with Audrey Hepburn in this film — and he doesn't even know that she's a princess.

18) Which Mel Brooks' film featured Zero Mostel and Gene Wilder?

19) What film featured Jack Lemmon and Sandy Dennis as a couple who run into a series of problems while travelling to New York?

20) A young and innocent Liza Minelli falls in love with Wendell Burton in this film.

21) Kirk Douglas stars in this film about a slave revolt in Rome. It was directed by Stanley Kubrick.

22) Lauren Bacall and Humphrey Bogart fell in love while filming this movie.

23) This movie featured Tony Curtis as the greatest magician of all time.

24) Name the comedy which featured Sophia Loren as Cary Grant's housekeeper.

25) Charles Grodin's marriage falls apart when he meets Cybill Shepard while on his honeymoon.

26) Name the film in which Shirley Temple played the mountain girl who has a difficult time adapting to city life.

27) Not many people realize that Gene Kelly directed this famous musical, which featured Barbra Streisand and Walter Mattheau.

28) This western featured Gary Cooper as a sheriff threatened by a gang of outlaws.

29) Steve McQueen, James Garner, and Richard Attenborough were among the many stars in this drama about allied P.O.W.'s in World War II.

30) What film features Elizabeth Taylor and Richard Burton as an artist and a married minister who fall in love?

31) In what film did George Segal and Barbra Streisand fall in love?

32) Al Pacino had his first starring role in this film about junkies in New York.

33) What musical featured Yves Montand as Barbra Streisand's psychiatrist?

34) What film featured Charles Laughton searching for prisoner Frederic March?

35) In this film, Sidney Portier helped a group of nuns build a chapel.

36) Dustin Hoffman once played the only survivor of the Battle of Little Big Horn. Can you name the film?

37) Katharine Hepburn starred in this version of Louisa May Alcott's classic novel.

38) What is the name of the World War II drama in which Cliff Robertson plays John F. Kennedy?

39) James Dean was set to star in this film when he had his tragic and fatal car accident. Paul Newman took the role about the life of boxer Rocky Graziano.

40) Orson Welles, Joseph Cotton, and Agnes Moorehead all made their debuts in this film.

41) This film about the marathon dance contests of the Depression starred Jane Fonda.

42) Name the film that made Errol Flynn a star.

43) A capsized ocean liner was the real star of this Irwin Allen movie.

44) What film featured Jessica Walter trying to murder disc jockey Clint Eastwood?

45) Peter Sellers played a fumbling detective in this hilarious comedy.

46) Robert De Niro was one of the many excellent actors to perform in this version of F. Scott Fitzgerald's novel.

47) Name the film biography which featured Dustin Hoffman as a brilliant but troubled comedian.

48) Jack Nicholson played a Navy police officer sent to pick up Randy Quaid in this film.

49) Steve McQueen starred in this film version of William Faulkner's novel.

50) Mia Farrow starred in Roman Polanski's look at modern witchcraft.

51) Mike Nichols directed Art Garfunkel and Jack Nicholson in this seminal '70s film.

52) Lee Marvin and Jane Fonda teamed up for this comedy-western.

53) Sam Peckinpah directed Steve McQueen and Ali McGraw in this violent cops and robbers film.

54) Peter Bogdanovich directed this movie about a boy growing up in a small Texas town in the '50s.

55) Aliens invade human bodies and turn them into pods in this classic sci-fi film.

56) Lousie Fletcher took home an Academy Award for her role as Nurse Ratchet in this film.

57) What was Elvis Presley's first film?

58) Ali McGraw and Ryan O'Neal starred in one of the most popular love stories of all time.

59) In this musical, Deborah Kerr played the tutor to the many children of the King of Siam.

60) Rebel Paul Newman clashes with father Melvyn Douglas in this film.

61) This movie about a killer on the run featured Ida Lupino and Humphrey Bogart.

62) Irving Berlin wrote the songs, and Fred Astaire and Bing Crosby danced to and sang them in this classic musical.

63) Robert Redford played a famous stunt-pilot of the '20s in this film of the same name.

64) Burt Lancaster and Kirk Douglas starred as Wyatt Earp and Doc Holliday in this classic western.

65) This famous war story featured Anthony Quinn, Gregory Peck, and David Niven among many other stars.

66) Jimmy Stewart played a famous big band leader in this bio-pic.

67) This comedy is remembered for the scene in which Charlie Chaplin eats his shoe.

68) Ronald Coleman starred in this version of Dicken's novel about the French Revolution.

69) Topol helped to bring the lives of Ukranian Jews alive on film in this popular musical.

70) Several bachelor brothers search for wives in this musical revue.

71) In this film, Anthony Quinn plays a passionate Greek and Alan Bates an uptight Englishman.

72) Charles Boyer slowly drives Ingrid Bergman mad until Jimmy Stewart comes along to save the day.

73) Jane Wyman won critical praise for her portrayal of a deaf-mute in this movie

74) Bing Crosby was awarded his first Academy Award for his portrayal of a priest in this film.

75) This adaptation of Hemingway's novel starred Ingrid Bergman and Gary Cooper.

76) Lynn Redgrave reached stardom for her portrayal of a homely English girl. Can you name the film?

77) Jayne Mansfield was the girl who just couldn't resist, and Little Richard and Eddie Cochran added musical support in this movie.

78) Ali McGraw and Richard Benjamin made their screen debut in this version of Philip Roth's novella.

79) This classic science fiction movie featured Leslie Nielson as a scientist with something to hide.

80) Todd Browning's cult classic about performers in a circus sideshow.

81) In this film, John Wayne led a squadron of fighting pilots against the Japanese during World War II.

82) After Rosalind Russell hires Fred MacMurray as her secretary, the two of them fall in love.

83) James Stewart is a photographer laid up in bed, and Grace Kelly is his girlfriend in this Hitchcock classic.

84) Name the seven films that Marlene Dietrich made for Josef von Sternberg.

85) In which musical did Doris Day make her debut?

86) Humphrey Bogart starred in six John Huston films. Can you name them?

87) Gene Hackman won an Academy Award for his portrayal of a detective fighting a drug smuggling operation in this film.

88) Alan Ladd played the title role in this classic western.

89) Billy Wilder directed Edward G. Robinson, Fred MacMurray, and Barbara Stanwyck in this classic film about murder and insurance fraud.

90) Francis Ford Coppola directed Gene Hackman in this classic study of paranoia.

91) What is the full title of the Stanley Kubrick film commonly referred to as *Dr. Strangelove*?

92) Can you name the films which featured Ronald Reagan and a chimpanzee?

93) Raymond Chandler, Howard Hawks, Humphrey Bogart, and Lauren Bacall teamed up for this complicated mystery.

94) Name the first silent movie to win an Academy Award.

95) Grace Kelly starred in three Alfred Hitchcock films. Can you name them?

96) What was the title of Bruce Lee's first Hollywood Kung-Fu film?

97) The most expensive black and white film ever produced, it starred John Wayne, Richard Burton, and Robert Mitchum.

98) Marlon Brando, Frank Sinatra, and Jean Simmons teamed up in this musical.

99) Charlie Chaplin teamed up with child actor Jackie Coogan in this hit film.

100) Name the films for which John Ford won his three best directing Oscars.

101) Joanne Woodward won an Academy Award for playing a woman with three personalities.

102) Marlon Brando and Lee Marvin starred in this classic motorcycle film.

103) James Mason starred as evil Captain Nemo in this Walt Disney version of Jules Verne's novel.

104) This film won all but one of the Academy Awards presented in 1939.

105) Director George Cukor only won one Oscar. What is the name of the film?

106) This classic is shown on television more often than any other film, making it the most watched movie of all time.

107) What Brooke Sheilds film was banned in England?

108) Farrah Fawcett and Raquel Welch shared a bed in this steamy 1970 film.

109) Hollywood columnist Hedda Hopper made an appearance in this classic film about Hollywood.

110) Jodie Foster starred as a rape victim in this gripping drama.

111) Henry Fonda, Lee J. Cobb, and a host of stars played jurists in this behind-the-scenes courtroom drama.

112) The Beatles starred in this animated classic.

113) Burt Lancaster, Dean Martin, and Jacqueline Bisset starred in this disaster movie — the first of its kind.

114) Germany's first talking picture, it was directed by Fritz Lang and starred Peter Lorre.

115) Name the film, set in the world of ballet, which featured Shirley MacLaine and Anne Bancroft.

116) Clark Gable, Charles Laughton, and Franchot Tone all received Academy Award nominations for their work in this "seafaring" film.

117) Alan Arkin played a deaf mute in this version of Carson McCuller's story.

118) Jose Ferrer played the classic hero in the original film version of this tale, Gerard Depardieu starred in the most recent version.

119) Fellini's classic about life in a seaside village coping with Fascism.

120) James Dean and Rock Hudson vie for Elizabeth Taylor's attention in this film about the oil business.

121) Stanley Kubrick directed Ryan O'Neal in this epic set in the 18th century.

122) Name the film which not only featured Arlo Guthrie, but was based on his hit song of the same name.

123) Cornel Wilde survived the challenges of the jungle in this film.

124) Gregory Peck and Lee Remick starred in what some consider to be the scariest film of all time.

125) Edward G. Robinson was considered a "menace to society" in this famous gangster film.

126) Sissy Spacek starred as country singer Loretta Lynn in this film.

127) John Hurt and Anthony Hopkins starred in David Lynch's film about deformed John Merrick.

128) This Woody Allen comedy featured a Japanese hero in search of a stolen recipe for egg salad.

129) Can you name the first Marx Brothers film?

130) Jayne Mansfield starred in this rock and roll film that featured performances by Little Richard, Fats Domino, and Eddie Cochran.

131) The word "damn" was first heard when Clark Gable said it at the close of *Gone With the Wind*. What was the second film to use the word?

132) Robert Redford directed Mary Tyler Moore, Timothy Hutton, and Donald Sutherland in this film about a family trying to cope with a tragedy.

133) Robert DeNiro and Harvey Kietel have a love-hate relationship in this Martin Scorcese-directed film.

134) Bill Haley's "Rock Around the Clock" was featured in the opening scene of this 1954 film.

135) Name the film starring Dick Van Dyke in which a whole town tries to quit smoking.

136) John Ford directed and John Wayne became a star as a result of his performance in this classic western.

137) Name the western which starred Warren Beatty and Julie Christie and was directed by Robert Altman.

138) Jack Nicholson and Marlon Brando first shared the screen in this western.

139) What was the only film to have featured Fred Astaire and Gene Kelly dancing together?

140) The horrifying shower sequence alone has made this Alfred Hitchcock film famous.

141) Woody Allen won an Academy Award for this filmed about a doomed love affair. Diane Keaton co-starred.

142) Bette Midler portrayed a Janis Joplin-like singer in this film about fame and abuse.

143) Harold Lloyd is perhaps best remembered for the scene in which he hangs from a clock atop a building. Can you name the film?

144) What are the names of the two Billy Wilder films which feature Marilyn Monroe?

145) Name the only film to be taken from one Nobel prize-winning novelist's book, and then adapted for the screen by another Nobel prize-winning novelist. Who are the writers?

146) This film was so successful that Quaker Oats named a candy bar after it and the book it was based on.

147) Bing Crosby starred in this adaptation of Mark Twain's story about a time traveler.

148) Paul Newman and George Kennedy starred in this great prison chain gang story.

149) William Bendix played a baseball hall of famer in this 1948 film biography.

150) Burt Reynolds and Jon Voight are among a group of men who take a canoe trip in Georgia.

151) Name the only film Marlon Brando both directed and starred in.

TRIVIA ANSWERS

ACTORS

1) John Gilbert
2) George Burns, age 80, *The Sunshine Boys*
3) Frank Sinatra
4) Frank Sinatra
5) Gene Hackman and Al Pacino
6) Robert Redford
7) Roy Scheider
8) Robert Culp and Elliott Gould
9) Melvyn Douglas
10) James Coburn
11) Sidney Poitier
12) Steve McQueen
13) Karl Malden
14) Walter Mattheau
15) Yves Montand
16) Alan Bates
17) John Travolta
18) Paul Scofield
19) Rod Steiger
20) Jon Voight
21) Michael Redgrave
22) Edward Albert
23) Alec Guiness
24) George Peppard
25) David Carradine
26) Sir Ralph Richardson

27) Paul Robeson
28) Maximilian Schell
29) Billy Dee Williams
30) Alec Guinness and Peter Sellers
31) Jack Palance
32) John Casavettes
33) Montgomery Clift
34) Jackie Coogan
35) Gary Cooper
36) Noel Coward
37) Burt Lancaster
38) Stan Laurel and Oliver Hardy
39) Boris Karloff
40) Buster Keaton
41) Dennis Hopper
42) Rock Hudson
43) Cary Grant
44) Alec Guinness
45) Richard Burton
46) Yul Brynner
47) Kirk Douglas
48) Clint Eastwood
49) Peter Finch
50) Henry Fonda
51) Clark Gable
52) Peter Lorre
53) James Cagney
54) Marlon Brando

55) Warren Beatty
56) Cary Grant
57) Donald Sutherland
58) Maurice Chevalier
59) Danny Kaye
60) Richard Dreyfus
61) Gene Kelly
62) Donald O'Connor
63) Mick Jagger
64) Warren Beatty
65) Wallace Beery
66) Orson Welles and Joseph Cotton
67) George C. Scott

ACTRESSES

1) Janet Leigh and Vera Miles
2) Hedy Lamarr
3) Donna Reed
4) Hattie McDaniel, for *Gone With the Wind*
5) Natalie Wood
6) Shirley MacLaine
7) Marilyn Monroe
8) Gena Rowlands
9) Liza Minelli
10) Doris Day
11) Rita Hayworth

12) Jane Russell and Marilyn Monroe
13) Shirley MacLaine
14) Barbra Streisand
15) Jill Clayburgh
16) Madeline Kahn
17) Shirley Jones
18) Judy Garland and Margaret O'Brien
19) Angela Lansbury
20) Talia Shire
21) Elizabeth Taylor
22) Natalie Wood
23) Liza Minelli
24) Margot Kidder
25) Cicely Tyson
26) Ruby Keeler
27) Patty Duke and Anne Bancroft
28) Ava Gardner
29) Patty Duke
30) Elizabeth Taylor
31) Sandy Dennis
32) Paula Prentiss
33) Angela Lansbury
34) Ruth Gordon
35) Jeanne Moreau
36) Ingrid Bergman
37) Claudette Colbert and Vivien Leigh
38) Simone Signoret
39) Eartha Kitt and Ella Fitzgerald

40) Diane Keaton
41) Jody Foster
42) Charlotte Rampling
43) Dorothy Lamour
44) Joan Fontaine
45) Olivia de Havilland
46) Claudette Colbert
47) Audrey Hepburn
48) Shirley Temple
49) Marilyn Monroe
50) Ellen Burstyn
51) Agnes Moorehead
52) Shelley Winters

MOVIES

1) *Smokey and the Bandit*
2) *The Godfather II*
3) *Beach Blanket Bingo*
4) *Blazing Saddles*
5) *Guess Who's Coming to Dinner?*
6) *Cat on a Hot Tin Roof*
7) *Catch-22*
8) *Shaft*
9) *Run Silent, Run Deep*
10) *Marty*
11) *Midnight Cowboy*

12) *The Man Who Fell to Earth*
13) *Live and Let Die*
14) *Love and Death*
15) *Saboteur*
16) *Robin and Marion*
17) *Roman Holiday*
18) *The Producers*
19) *The Out of Towners*
20) *The Sterile Cuckoo*
21) *Spartacus*
22) *To Have and Have Not*
23) *Houdini*
24) *Houseboat*
25) *The Heartbreak Kid*
26) *Heidi*
27) *Hello Dolly*
28) *High Noon*
29) *The Great Escape*
30) *The Sandpipers*
31) *The Owl and the Pussycat*
32) *Panic in Needle Park*
33) *On a Clear Day You Can See Forever*
34) *Les Miserables*
35) *Lillies of the Field*
36) *Little Big Man*
37) *Little Women*
38) *PT109*
39) *Somebody Up There Likes Me*

40) *Citizen Kane*
41) *They Shoot Horses Don't They*
42) *Captain Blood*
43) *The Poseidon Adventure*
44) *Play Misty For Me*
45) *The Pink Panther*
46) *The Last Tycoon*
47) *Lenny*
48) *The Last Detail*
49) *The Reivers*
50) *Rosemary's Baby*
51) *Carnal Knowledge*
52) *Cat Ballou*
53) *The Getaway*
54) *The Last Picture Show*
55) *Invasion of the Body Snatchers*
56) *One Flew Over the Cuckoo's Nest*
57) *Love Me Tender*
58) *Love Story*
59) *The King and I*
60) *Hud*
61) *High Sierra*
62) *Holiday Inn*
63) *The Great Waldo Pepper*
64) *Gunfight at OK Corral*
65) *The Guns of Navarrone*
66) *The Glen Miller Story*
67) *The Gold Rush*

68) *Tale of Two Cities*
69) *Fiddler on the Roof*
70) *Seven Brides for Seven Brothers*
71) *Zorba the Greek*
72) *Gaslight*
73) *Johnny Belinda*
74) *Going My Way*
75) *For Whom the Bell Tolls*
76) *Gregory Girl*
77) *The Girl Can't Help It*
78) *Goodbye Columbus*
79) *Forbidden Planet*
80) *Freaks*
81) *Flying Tigers*
82) *Take a Letter, Darling*
83) *Rear Window*
84) *The Blue Angel, Morocco, Dishonored, Shanghai Express, Blond Venus, The Scarlet Empress, The Devil is a Woman*
85) *Romance on the High Seas*
86) *Beat the Devil, Across the Pacific, Key Largo, The African Queen, The Maltese Falcon, The Treasure of the Sierra Madre*
87) *The French Connection*
88) *Shane*
89) *Double Indemnity*
90) *The Conversation*

91) *Dr. Stranglove, or How I Learned to Stop Worrying and Love the Bomb*
92) *Bedtime for Bonzo, Bonzo Goes to College*
93) *The Big Sleep*
94) *Wings*
95) *Dial M for Murder, Rear Window, To Catch a Thief*
96) *Enter the Dragon*
97) *The Longest Day*
98) *Guys and Dolls*
99) *The Kid*
100) *The Grapes of Wrath, How Green Was My Valley, The Quiet Man*
101) *The Three Faces of Eve*
102) *The Wild Ones*
103) *20,000 Leagues Under the Sea*
104) *Gone With the Wind*
105) *My Fair Lady*
106) *Casablanca*
107) *Pretty Baby*
108) *Myra Breckinridge*
109) *Sunset Boulevard*
110) *The Accused*
111) *Twelve Angry Men*
112) *Yellow Submarine*
113) *Airport*
114) *M*
115) *The Turning Point*

143) *Safety Last*
144) *The Seven Year Itch, Some Like it Hot*
145) *To Have and Have Not.* Ernest Hemingway and William Faulkner.
146) *Willy Wonka and the Chocolate Factory*
147) *A Connecticut Yankee in King Arthur's Court*
148) *Cool Hand Luke*
149) *The Babe Ruth Story*
150) *Deliverance*
151) *One-Eyed Jacks*